## EARLY THEMES

# Neighborhood and Community

by Kathleen M. Hollenbeck

UNIV OF MOUNT UNION
CURRICULUM CENTER

SCHOLASTIC
**PROFESSIONAL BOOKS**

NEW YORK • TORONTO • LONDON • AUCKLAND • SYDNEY
MEXICO CITY • NEW DELHI • HONG KONG • BUENOS AIRES

*To Kimber Lee, who no longer lives in my neighborhood,*
*but always remains in my heart. BFF!*

"Ice Cream Man" by Sandra Liatsos is copyrighted by the author and used by permission of Marian Reiner for the author.

The student pages in this book may be reproduced for classroom use. No other part of this publication may be reproduced in whole or in part, or stored in a retrieval system, or transmitted in any form or by any means, electronic, mechanical, photocopying, recording, or otherwise, without written permission of the publisher. For information regarding permission, write to Scholastic Inc., 557 Broadway, New York, NY 10012.

Edited by Joan Novelli
Cover design by Maria Lilja
Cover art by Jo Lynn Alcorn
Interior design by Solutions by Design, Inc.
Interior illustrations by James Graham Hale
Poster design by Kathy Massaro
Poster art by Jane Conteh-Morgan

ISBN 0-439-22255-9

Copyright © 2003 by Kathleen M. Hollenbeck
Published by Scholastic Inc.
All rights reserved. Printed in the U.S.A.

2 3 4 5 6 7 8 9 10    40    09 07 06 05 04 03

# Contents

# About This Book

During the early years, children spend most of their time at home or close by. Their knowledge and perspective are shaped by interactions with the people, places, and things they most often see. As a result, the study of home and community is an integral part of primary curriculums across the nation, helping children to better understand themselves and the world they live in and providing a basic building block from which all other learning can extend.

Through hands-on activities, poetry, and children's literature, this resource book introduces and reinforces concepts central to the study of neighborhood and community. Because the book is geared for young learners, it begins with an emphasis on the home, progresses to a study of the neighborhood, and then moves on to an understanding of what makes up a community.

The activities provided incorporate all major subject areas and support curriculum standards developed by the National Council for the Social Studies and by a sampling of states across the United States. Standards touched on include, for example, that children will examine the interaction of people and their environment, demonstrate an understanding of past and present, and explore ways in which people design homes, work space, and play space to reflect their needs, ideas, personalities, and culture.

## WHAT'S INSIDE

Here are some of the teaching materials you'll find in this book:

◎ **Launching the Theme:** activities for introducing the unit, getting a sense of what children know, and building excitement for what they'll learn

◎ **Learning Center Links:** ideas for setting up an appealing, educational learning center based on the theme of neighborhood and community

◎ **Hands-on Activities:** step-by-step directions for guiding students in activities that connect every aspect of the curriculum, including math, science, social studies, language arts, music, art, and drama

◎ **Reproducible Activity Pages:** more than a dozen age-appropriate, interactive reproducible pages designed to deepen children's understanding and promote hands-on learning

◎ **Literature Connections:** book suggestions with related activities to enrich learning

◎ **Neighborhood and Community Celebration:** suggestions for wrapping up the unit and celebrating children's learning

◎ **"I Am a Community Helper:"** a colorful, interactive poster that highlights people and places in a community, and incorporates teaching activities

## WHY TEACH WITH THEMES?

Themes integrate core skills with discovery. They allow children to revisit a topic again and again, examining it from all angles and within all subject areas, strengthening skills across the curriculum while deepening understanding, bolstering retention, building excitement, and motivating children to learn.

Themes offer structure and direction, a detailed game plan for a certain goal. With thematic teaching, you and your students can focus on a topic and explore it in depth without sacrificing the skills you're required to teach. Excited and eager to learn, your students will participate and long remember the lessons you teach.

## GETTING READY

Consider the following suggestions to help you get the most from your thematic unit:

◎ **Materials:** Each lesson contains a list of materials required for completing the activity. Look over the lists well in advance to be sure you have or can get what you need prior to presenting the lesson. You may want to inform families of your theme, opening the door for contributions from home.

◎ **Grouping:** Many of the lessons invite children to work in pairs or small groups. Create these groups each time the need arises or establish them at the start, keeping them intact for the duration of

the unit. If you choose to set up long-term groups, promote a cooperative atmosphere by allowing group members to create their own name and logo.

◎ **Assessment:** Thematic units offer many opportunities to assess student comprehension and development. As children draw maps and act out the roles of community workers, you will be able to gauge their understanding of the topic. Store children's work in manila folders, decorated by students and labeled with their names (and group logos, if applicable).

## SETTING UP A LEARNING CENTER

Give your classroom a hometown feeling with a learning center built around neighborhood and community. Friendly and familiar, community sights such as homes, schools, and shops evoke in children a sense of warmth and security. Regardless of its theme, though, a good learning center requires a few basic ingredients to make it work well. A small table, several chairs, a bookshelf, and wall space form the foundation of a successful learning station. In addition, consider the following tips:

◎ **Decorate the Center:** Rugs, pillows, beanbag chairs, and stuffed animals go a long way toward making a learning center the place where children want to be. Tailor yours to fit the community theme by adding dolls or puppets of neighborhood workers, brochures from sights around the community, and plenty of picture books featuring rural, urban, and suburban neighborhoods.

◎ For visual intrigue, hang a collage of magazine photos depicting parks, restaurants, playgrounds, and other familiar community sights.

◎ **Make It Their Center:** Be sure children view the learning center as their place to go to learn more about neighborhood and community, share what they've learned, and display their knowledge. Encourage them to share free time there, participating in the Learning Center activities suggested throughout this book and immersing themselves in the theme.

# PROFESSIONAL RESOURCES

## Books

*Thematic Poetry: Neighborhoods and Communities* by Betsy Franco (Scholastic, 2000). This resource provides more than 30 poems relating to neighborhood topics and geared for young readers.

*Thematic Poetry: Transportation* by Betsy Franco (Scholastic, 2001). Getting around has never seemed as fun as it does in these poems about cars, trains, and other kinds of transportation.

*Seeing the Whole Through Social Studies* by Terry Lindquist (Heinemann, 1995). An experienced teacher and curriculum writer, Terry Lindquist presents her ideas on reorganizing the social studies curriculum to promote more meaningful learning.

*Ways That Work: Putting Social Studies Standards Into Practice* by Terry Lindquist (Heinemann, 1997). The author provides teachers with creative strategies to meet social studies standards.

## Web Sites

Recycle City (**http://www.epa.gov.recyclecity /mainmap.htm**): This fun, interactive Web site presents a make-believe city scene for children to explore, navigating their way around city streets while learning the value of recycling.

Earth Day on Your Block (**http://www.allspecies.org/neigh /blocka.htm**): Children can make a difference by starting an Earth Day celebration in their neighborhood.

# Launching the Theme

**A**s children grow, they rely on familiar sights to tell them where they are in time and space. Passing a local market, they realize they're almost home. They know that a post office is a place to mail letters and a restaurant offers meals. Knowing these things builds a feeling of comfort and security. It conveys the message "You belong here. This is where you live." Use the activities that follow to launch your study of neighborhood and community, guiding children from their front doors into the world that surrounds them.

## BACKGROUND NOTES

Around the world, all people share the same set of basic human needs. These include the need for food, drinkable water, clothing, shelter, and love. Homes and families meet these needs, and they are helped by the goods and services found within a community.

# Build a Neighborhood Word Wall

**Children use words related to the theme to make a word wall for their classroom.**

## Materials

- ◎ sentence strips or index cards
- ◎ thick permanent marker
- ◎ stapler
- ◎ scissors

## Teaching the Lesson

**1** Find out what children already know about the theme. Ask: "What is a neighborhood? What is a community?"

**2** As children share ideas, record words they use that tell something about neighborhoods and communities—for example, *home*, *store*, and *sidewalk*.

**3** Display the words on a bulletin board or wall and add a title. As children progress through the unit, help them add more words to the wall.

**4** To add visual clues, invite children to cut out pictures from magazines that illustrate the words. Have them place the pictures next to the corresponding words.

---

**ACTIVITY Extension** Write the following poem on sentence strips and display it in a pocket chart. Ask children to insert their own words or prewritten words to complete the poem. Suggested words include *post office*, *fire station*, *school*, *church*, *library*, *bank*, and *store*.

**What Do I See?**

What do I see
As I walk down the street
In my city or town
On my very own feet?

I see a _____
And a _____, too.
I see a _____.
There is so much to do!

---

## Learning Center Link

*Laminate and cut out the community cards on page 10. Place them in an envelope. During free time, let students sort the cards to show what takes place at each location. Invite children to add their own activity strips as well, naming additional activities that occur at each location. For a language arts twist, provide lined paper, and ask children to list the verbs they find on the cards.*

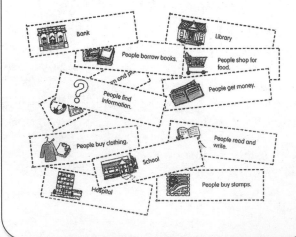

# From Home to Community

**Children make a book they can add to as they progress through the unit and learn about neighborhood and community.**

## Materials

- ◎ theme stationery (page 11)
- ◎ crayons or markers
- ◎ colored paper squares (optional)
- ◎ stapler
- ◎ scissors

## Teaching the Lesson

1. Give each child multiple copies of page 11. Have children stack the pages and staple them to make a book.

2. As children complete each of the four main sections of the theme unit (Home Is a Special Place, Walk Around the Neighborhood, What Makes a Community?, People Live and Work in a Community), ask them to represent that part of the unit with a drawing or a mosaic (a picture made by gluing on half-inch, precut squares of paper to form a design, such as that of a house or arrangement of homes or stores in a neighborhood). Encourage children to write or dictate a sentence to go with each picture.

3. Invite children to share the completed books with family members at home.

**ACTIVITY Extension**

Bring in a map of the community in which your school is located. Help children identify familiar places around town, such as the library, post office, or town hall. If your town does not have a child-friendly map to share, take out chart paper and invite children to name some of their favorite places in the community. Pass out drawing paper, and assign each child one place from the list to illustrate and label. Display the pictures on a classroom or hall wall, adding details (roads, signs, and so on) to create a map.

**Literature Connection**

Read Melrose Cooper's *I Got Community* (Henry Holt, 1995), a poetic presentation of the ways people in a community depend on each other. As a class, create an extension to the book, highlighting people in the community who contribute to children's lives in some way. Children can illustrate a person of choice and write or dictate a sentence in Cooper's spry dialect, beginning, "I got a..."

## Learning Center Link

*Place a board game or two in the learning center to reinforce community sights. Rivers, Roads, and Rails (Ravensburger–F.X. Schmid), provides colorful tiles children can move and match to build roads, railroad tracks, and waterways. Parker Brothers' Clue Jr. turns players into young detectives as they search a neighborhood for missing toys and pets.*

# Community Cards

 Post Office

 People learn and play.

 Hospital

 People borrow books.

 School

 Babies are born.

 Library

 People get money.

 Bank

 People buy clothing.

 Store

 People read and write.

 People mail letters.

 People find information.

 Doctors help people feel better.

 People buy stamps.

 People deposit money.

 People shop for food.

*Early Themes: Neighborhood and Community*  Scholastic Professional Books

Name_____ Date _____

# Home Is a Special Place

**H**ome is the center of a young child's world. It is the first place children see as they open their eyes every morning and the last place they glimpse before nodding off at night. In this section, you'll find activities designed to help children answer the questions "What is a home?" and "What needs do people in a home help meet?" Children will consider various kinds of homes and will describe their own homes in different ways.

## BACKGROUND NOTES

The family home comes in many shapes and sizes. From mobile homes to mansions, people choose homes that fit their needs, budgets, lifestyles, and tastes. Some of the homes people live in include apartments, condominiums, and one- or two-family houses.

# This Is My Home

**Children make mini-books to show what their homes look like and who lives there.**

## Materials

- ◎ unlined white paper (8 ½- by 11-inches)
- ◎ crayons or colored pencils
- ◎ scissors
- ◎ stapler

## Teaching the Lesson

**1** For each child, cut a sheet of paper into four equal sections. Stack the sections and staple twice along the left side to make a book.

**2** Have children write "This Is My Home" and their name on the first page, to serve as a cover.

**3** Ask children to draw pictures in their books, illustrating what their home looks like and who lives there. Children's drawings may reflect different areas of their home—for example, some might draw the exterior, while others may prefer to show a favorite room.

**ACTIVITY Extension** Have children draw a picture of something they enjoy doing at home, such as playing with toys or baking cookies with a parent. Let children share their pictures and guess each other's activities.

**Literature Connection** Read *A House Is a House for Me* by Mary Ann Hoberman (Viking, 1978). Brainstorm other ways something can be a "house"— for example, a mitten is a house for a cold hand, a sock for a foot, and a cabinet for a box of crackers.

## Learning Center Link

*Provide colorful magazines, scissors, glue, and construction paper. Invite children to visit the center during free time to make collages of homes, showing what's inside and outside a home, such as bedrooms, living rooms, kitchens, outdoor gardens, and so on.*

# Map Your Room

**Children learn early mapping skills by mapping the layout of their bedrooms.**

## Materials

- ◎ paper (colored or white, 8 ½- by 11-inches or larger)
- ◎ crayons or markers

## Teaching the Lesson

**1** Draw the shape of the classroom on the chalkboard. With children's help, draw the location of various components of the room—for example, the door, children's cubbies, your desk, a reading rug, the closets, and the windows. Add small squares or circles to indicate placement of desks or tables. Explain that the drawing you have just made is a classroom map.

2. Provide paper and ask children to map the layout of their bedrooms (or another room) at home. They may be able to do this from memory, or they may need to take the paper home and complete the map there.

**Literature Connection**
Use *Mapping Penny's World*, by Loreen Leedy (Henry Holt, 2000), to explore the use of map keys. Let children study the map of Lisa's bedroom. Then point to the map key. Invite children to identify each item on the key and locate it on the map. Do this for other maps in the book as well. Then work together to create a map and key for the playground, cafeteria, or other area of the school.

## Learning Center Link

*Draw several basic maps to show the layout of individual rooms in a make-believe home. Draw a key to go with each one. Laminate the maps and keys, and place them in the learning center with a stack of lined 3- by 5-inch index cards. During free time, children can study a map and its key and write questions for classmates to answer, such as "What is closest to the bookshelf?"*

# Window Math

**Children read a poem about a house with many windows and add felt windows to a flannel board display.**

## Materials

- flannel board
- felt strips (in one solid color)
- adhesive labels
- yellow felt
- "Window Math" reproducible (page 17)

## Teaching the Lesson

1. On a flannel board, use felt strips to outline the walls and rooms of a house.

2. Apply small adhesive labels to mark the different rooms mentioned in the poem. Cut out 12 yellow felt rectangles to serve as windows.

3. Give each child a copy of page 17, and read the poem aloud together. Then read it again, slowly. Invite volunteers to put the windows in place on the flannel board as they are mentioned in the poem.

**ACTIVITY Extension** Give each child an 8½- by 11-inch sheet of white construction paper and a 4-by-11-inch strip of yellow construction paper. Have children cut 12 equal rectangles out of the yellow paper (or give them precut rectangles). Ask them to glue the 12 windows on the white paper (to represent a home) and write a number sentence to go with it.

**Literature Connection** Read aloud *Goodnight, Goodnight*, by Eve Rice (Greenwillow, 1980). This book is out of print, but is still available in many libraries and provides an excellent peek into windows around a city as people and pets get ready to settle down for the night. Ask children to describe what each window reveals about the different person(s) or pet(s) behind it.

## Learning Center Link

*Place a journal in the learning center. Ask each child to complete one page during free time, writing and drawing what they see when they look through a window at home.*

LANGUAGE ARTS

# A Sense of Home

**Children and their families complete a take-home reproducible, describing how their home feels, smells, looks, sounds, and tastes.**

## Materials

◉ "A Sense of Home" reproducible (page 18)

# Teaching the Lesson

**1** Give each child a copy of page 18 to take home.

**2** Encourage children to enlist the help of family members to describe in words and pictures how their homes feel, smell, look, sound, and taste.

**3** Invite children to share their sensory "pictures" of home with the class. What are some favorite sensory connections children have of their homes?

**ACTIVITY Extension** Invite children to bring in an example of something sensory from home: something they can see, taste, feel, touch, or smell. Categorize the samples as students share them.

**Literature Connection** Read *What You Know First*, by Patricia MacLachlan (Joanna Cotler Books, 1995), a poetic reflection on what makes home a familiar place to be. Invite children to put themselves in the main character's place and describe four special details they would remember about their current home or community if they had to move away.

## Learning Center Link

*Have children cut out pictures from magazines and either make a sensory collage of sights, sounds, smells, and tastes of home or glue the pictures in columns to show where in their own homes they would find each pictured item.*

# Word Family Homes

**This interactive bulletin board lets children sort word families into different types of dwellings.**

## Materials

- ◎ tagboard strips (or sentence strips)
- ◎ craft paper
- ◎ thick permanent marker
- ◎ tape

## Teaching the Lesson

**1** Write words from various word families—for example, from the *-op* family, the *-ig* family, and the *-un* family—on 4-inch strips of tagboard. Write four words from each family.

**2** From craft paper, cut out patterns that represent several different kinds of homes, such as an apartment building, a duplex, and a mobile home. Display these on a bulletin board or wall in the classroom.

**3** Ask children to identify the various kinds of dwellings and help you assign each home the name of a different word family. The apartment building, for example, might be the future home of the *-ug* family. Have children sort the word cards and tape

them on the appropriate homes. Use blank tagboard strips for children to write and post additional words.

 **Literature Connection** Cynthia Rylant's *Bunny Bungalow* (Harcourt, 1999) offers an adorable look at the ways a family turns an empty house into a home. Invite children to read the book with you. Then go back in search of words that reflect a cozy home, such as quilts, rocking chair, and tubs. Ask children to think of and share favorite images from their own homes.

**ACTIVITY Extension** Cut out additional dwellings to add to your word-family display. Invite children to think of new word families. Label the homes, post them, and have children help you think of words that can "move in" to their new homes. Encourage children to be on the lookout for other words they hear or read that they can add to the existing word family homes.

## Learning Center Link

*How do children help out at home?* Use a jar graph to find out. Think of six common chores children might do, such as make their beds, put away toys, or set the table. Write each chore on a separate adhesive label and apply it to an empty peanut butter jar. Place the jars in a row beside a bowl of craft sticks and fine-tip permanent markers. Have children visit the learning center and note which chores they do at home. To indicate which chores they perform, have them write their names on individual craft sticks and place the sticks in the appropriate jars. At the end of the week, help children tally the results and record them on a picture graph.

# Window Math

My home has lots of windows.

Twelve in all, you see.

Two in the kitchen,

One in the den,

And two in my bedroom with me.

One in the bathroom,

Two in my mom's room,

Two in my brother's room, too.

One on each side of our only front door;

I have all these to look through.

—Kathleen M. Hollenbeck

*Early Themes: Neighborhood and Community  Scholastic Professional Books*

# A Sense of Home

What do I see in my home?

_____

_____

What do I smell in my home?

_____

_____

What do I taste in my home?

_____

_____

What do I touch in my home?

_____

_____

What do I hear in my home?

_____

_____

*Early Themes: Neighborhood and Community* Scholastic Professional Books

# Walk Around the Neighborhood

**L**ike home, a neighborhood can offer a sense of security, belonging, and familiarity. As children spend time outdoors in their neighborhoods, they come to know their unique characteristics: streets, parks, buildings, people, plant life, even congestion or noise. The activities in this section will help children to explore the sights, sounds, and makeup of their neighborhood and to identify and compare urban, suburban, and rural neighborhoods.

## BACKGROUND NOTES

A neighborhood is the local area around a person's home. In suburban areas, this might include rows of homes or apartments, sidewalks, and perhaps a park and a few stores. In urban areas, the word "neighborhood" often refers to an entire section of a city or town, which is quite often linked with the predominant ethnic heritage of those who live there.

# I Live in a Neighborhood

**Children identify and explore the sights they see in their neighborhoods.**

## Materials

◎ "I Live in a Neighborhood" reproducible (page 23)

◎ pencils

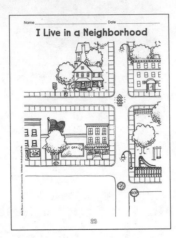

## Teaching the Lesson

**1** Invite children to name some of the sights they see in their neighborhoods—for example, high-rise buildings, houses, a park, stores, a bridge, or a brook.

**2** Give each child a copy of page 23. Ask children to study the picture and circle sights that are part of their neighborhoods.

**3** Encourage children to think of sights that they see in their neighborhoods but do not find on the activity page. Have them add those to the picture.

**Literature Connection** Read *My Perfect Neighborhood*, by Leah Komaiko (HarperCollins, 1990), in which a young girl describes her neighborhood—with added flair. Urge children to use Komaiko's approach in pictures and/or words, describing the school neighborhood they just explored, yet embellishing it.

**ACTIVITY Extension** If possible, take children on a short walk around the neighborhood surrounding their school. Encourage them to observe carefully the sights and sounds around them. Back in the classroom, make a graph listing what they saw and how many children recalled seeing each object or location.

## Learning Center Link

*Fill an empty soup can or other container with 20 or more craft sticks on which you have written neighborhood words such as* sidewalk, house, park, driveway, *and* elevator. *Wrap the can in craft paper and label it "Our Neighborhood Words." During free time, let children pull several sticks from the can and use them to write a sentence or story about a real or imagined neighborhood. Display the sentences (and accompanying illustrations) in and around the learning center.*

# The Mapping Mat

**Children follow directions to place colored marking pieces in a pattern across a neighborhood map.**

## Materials

◎ "The Mapping Mat" reproducible (page 24)

◎ colored marking chips (at least 20 per child, contained in empty margarine tubs)

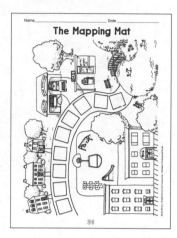

## Teaching the Lesson

**1** Give each child a copy of page 24. Have children listen carefully (without doing anything else) as you read the following set of directions:

*You are visiting a friend.*

*"Come with me!" your friend says. "Let's explore my neighborhood!"*

*Use your finger to trace the sidewalk from the very first house to the duck pond. Choose two different-colored marking chips. Place these on the first two steps on the sidewalk. This is the beginning of your sidewalk stepping pattern. Now randomly choose another marking chip from the container. If you pick the color that comes next in your pattern, place it on the sidewalk. If it is not the right color, put the chip back in the container and try again. Count how many tries it takes you to make a pattern on the sidewalk from the first house to the duck pond.*

**2** Read aloud the story a second time. Ask children to place markers on the mats as the story directs.

**ACTIVITY Extension** Create an errand list that children can follow on their story mats, using colored marking chips. For example, you might say, "Go with your dad to get gas. Leave a red chip there. Then run to the playground for a quick swing. Leave a green chip there. Visit your aunt in the first house on the street. Leave a blue chip there. Next, walk to the water and feed the ducks. Leave two red chips there." You might also encourage children to create their own course of events, placing chips at various locations as they tell a partner where they are going in the neighborhood and why.

**Literature Connection** Read aloud Deborah Chandra's *Miss Mabel's Table* (Harcourt Brace, 1994). Allow plenty of time for children to study the pictures in Miss Mabel's neighborhood as she leaves her home and travels to her restaurant: the workers she passes, the buildings and subway, the city waking up to a morning's activity. Pay close attention to the final illustrations in the book, which show Miss Mabel's table as it fits into the neighborhood scene.

## Learning Center Link

*Stock the learning center with drawing paper and crayons. Invite children to draw pictures of favorite people in their neighborhoods and to write or dictate sentences that tell about them. Bind the pictures to make a Favorite Neighbors scrapbook.*

# Neighborhood Scavenger Hunt

**Children and their families work together to describe their neighborhood from a mathematical perspective—noting quantity and size relationships.**

## Materials

◎ "Neighborhood Scavenger Hunt" reproducible (page 25)

## Teaching the Lesson

1 Give each child a copy of page 25. Have children complete the scavenger hunt activity with their families and then bring the reproducible back to school.

2 When all or most of the children have brought back the pages, graph the results to help children gain perspective on the kinds of neighborhoods that make up their community.

**ACTIVITY Extension**
Ask children and their families to draw a map of their own streets, showing the layout of homes, buildings, shops, natural landforms (rivers, forests), farms, and so on. Display the maps to create an overall look at children's neighborhoods.

**Literature Connection**
Read *Sidewalk Trip*, by Patricia Hubbell (HarperFestival, 1999), a story set in verse and filled with the sights and sounds of a city neighborhood. Ask children to think of something they might see if they were to take a similar walk through their own neighborhoods. Have children illustrate what they might see and write or dictate a four-line verse to describe the sights. (The verse does not have to rhyme.)

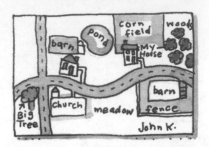

## Learning Center Link

*Use neighborhood sights to reinforce phonics skills. Cut out pictures from magazines to show things you might see in a neighborhood, such as trees, a park, and a school. Have children sort the pictures according to a phonics skill you want to reinforce. For example, to reinforce a study of blends, you might have children sort words into these categories: words beginning with* tr *(tree, truck),* fl *(flower garden, florist), and so on.*

# I Live in a Neighborhood

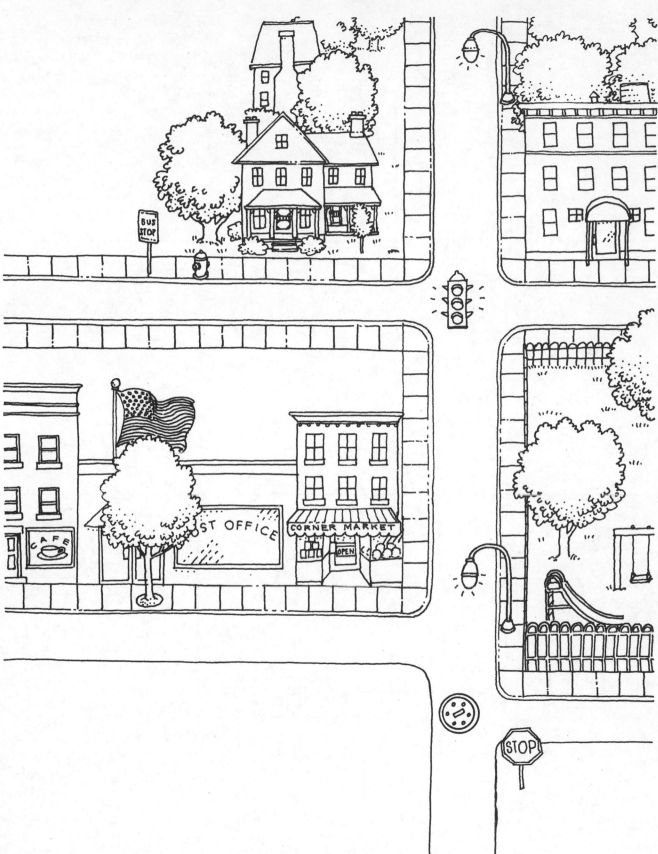

*Early Themes: Neighborhood and Community*  Scholastic Professional Books

# The Mapping Mat

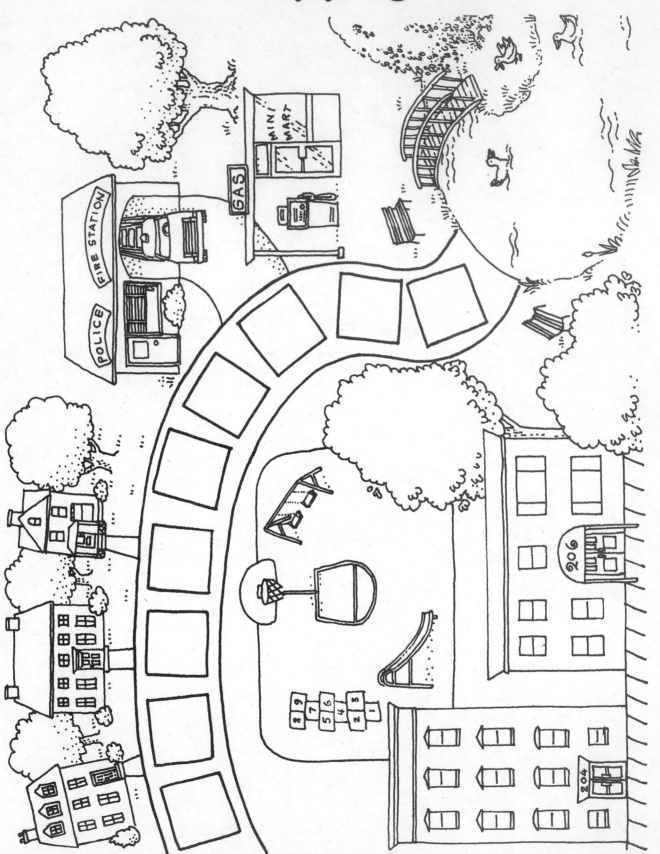

*Early Themes: Neighborhood and Community* Scholastic Professional Books

24

# Neighborhood Scavenger Hunt

Go on a scavenger hunt in your neighborhood! Take an adult family member with you. Look for answers to the questions below. Write the answers on the lines.

◎ Stand in front of your home.
   Count as many homes as you
   can see from where you stand.
   How many homes did you count?  _ _ _ _ _ _ _ _ _ _ _ _

◎ How many driveways do you
   see on your side of the street?  _ _ _ _ _ _ _ _ _ _ _ _

◎ Find the home on your street that
   has the most windows on the front.
   What color is the home?  _ _ _ _ _ _ _ _ _ _ _ _

◎ Look at the home beside yours.
   Is your home larger, smaller,
   or about the same size?  _ _ _ _ _ _ _ _ _ _ _ _

◎ Look at the colors of the homes or
   other buildings on your street.
   How many different colors do
   you see?  _ _ _ _ _ _ _ _ _ _ _ _

◎ Find something else to count
   on your street. What is it?
   How many did you count?  _ _ _ _ _ _ _ _ _ _ _ _

*Early Themes: Neighborhood and Community*  Scholastic Professional Books

# What Makes a Community?

S ome say it takes a village to raise a child—but what's in a village? In this section, children explore the content of a community and see how it meets their needs and the needs of others. On a very basic level, children will also examine the interaction of people with their natural environment and will discover ways in which community life is affected by science and technology.

## BACKGROUND NOTES

The presence of natural landforms— a pond, an ocean, a mountain range— greatly affects life in a community. Landforms influence such factors as a community's recreational activities, population, tourism, economy, and water supply.

# Build a Community

**Children cut out a variety of community buildings and display them on a mural.**

## Materials

- construction paper
- craft paper
- scissors
- markers

## Teaching the Lesson

1. Talk with children about buildings they see in their city or town—for example, homes, schools, banks, stores, and restaurants. List the buildings as children name them.

2. Invite children to cut out shapes from construction paper to create their own buildings.

3. Cover a bulletin board with craft paper and have children arrange their buildings on it.

4. Invite children to add people, trees, streets, sidewalks, and other details to complete the display.

 **ACTIVITY Extension** Ask children to name places they've visited in their community within the past week, such as the grocery store, post office, and dentist. List these on the left side of a chart. On the right side, write the reasons people go to each place—for example, to buy food, to mail letters, and to have a checkup.

**Literature Connection** For a glimpse of communities around the world, share Megan McDonald's *My House Has Stars* (Orchard Books, 1996). Help children locate each community on a world map and discuss ways life there resembles or differs from life in their city or town.

## Learning Center Link

Take at least 10 photographs of various places in the community around your school. Number the pictures and place them in a file folder along with a stack of index cards on which you have written needs, such as "I need to put gas in my car." During free time, have children match each need to the place in the community that meets it.

# Science in My Community

**Children cut out and assemble a wheel that demonstrates ways in which advances in communications, transportation, manufacturing, and use of energy affect community life.**

## Materials

◎ "Science in My Community" reproducibles (pages 31–32)

◎ brass fasteners

## Teaching the Lesson

1. Talk with children about ways their lives are affected by communication (television, radio, computer, Internet), transportation, manufacturing, and use of energy (electricity, gas, oil). For example, e-mail might allow a child to correspond often with a grandparent.

2. Give each child a copy of pages 31 and 32. Have children cut out and assemble the wheels, placing wheel A on top of wheel B and using a brass fastener to hold the two together.

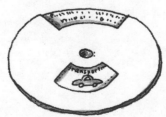

3. Have children turn the wheel slowly and read the text. Invite them to share examples from their own lives that highlight the contribution or effect of each technology listed.

**ACTIVITY Extension** Invite children to draw a picture to answer the question "How might our community be different 20 years from now, when you are grown up?"

**Literature Connection** Give children historical perspective with Angela Johnson's *Those Building Men* (Blue Sky Press, 2001), a graceful tribute to the men whose backbreaking efforts helped build and connect America's cities.

## Learning Center Link

*Contact the public library or local historical society to obtain books, copies of photographs, or other materials that show children what their community looked like long ago. Display these in the learning center for children to examine during free time.*

# Our Errand Lists

Children work in teams to determine where they would go to take care of items on a list of fictitious errands.

## Materials

◎ "Our Errand Lists" reproducible (page 33)

## Teaching the Lesson

1 Make enough copies of page 33 so that there is one errand list for every two children.

2 Divide the class into pairs. Give each pair one of the four errand lists.

3 Have partners work together to determine where they might need to go in a community to accomplish each errand. Have them write their answers in the designated spaces.

4 Bring the class together to talk about the errands and to discuss the places people go to accomplish them. Is there sometimes more than one place to go for an errand?

**ACTIVITY Extension** Help children draw very simple maps of make-believe communities, featuring at least four sites, such as a library, store, school, and doctor's office. Then have them make errand lists for classmates to follow, assigning tasks such as "Get a new book to read," or "Shop for a new pair of sneakers."

**Literature Connection** Yumi Heo's *One Afternoon* (Orchard Books, 1994) serves as a nice complement to this lesson. The focus of the story is a young boy running errands with his mother. After reading the story, have children write an errand list that Minho and his mother might have followed that day.

## Learning Center Link

*Introduce* Bunny Money *(International Playthings), a board game that invites children to run errands around a quaint little neighborhood.*

# Transportation in the Community

**Children read and work with a poem about transportation.**

## Materials

◎ "Getting Around" reproducible (page 34)

◎ pocket chart

◎ sentence strips

## Teaching the Lesson

1. Write each line of the poem on a sentence strip and place it in a pocket chart.

2. On shorter sentence strip pieces, draw pictures for transportation words such as *bus* or *car*.

3. Give each child a copy of page 34. Read the poem twice. Ask children to find the words that name forms of transportation.

4. Make a rebus by asking children to place the pictures in the pocket chart over the words they depict.

**ACTIVITY Extension** How do the children in your class travel to school each day? Graph the number of children who take the bus, ride in a car, ride on a bicycle, and walk. You might also want to graph other aspects of transportation, such as the kinds of vehicles families use: minivans, compact cars, motorcycles, station wagons, and so on.

**Literature Connection** Explore the many means of moving around with *Ways to Go*, an early reader by Dana Meachen Rau (Compass Point Books, 2001).

 **Learning Center Link**

*On a sentence strip, write the questions "What is your favorite way to travel? Why?" Laminate the strip and place it in a file folder with an ample supply of plain white paper. Ask children to answer the questions in words and pictures.*

# Science in My Community

**Wheel A**

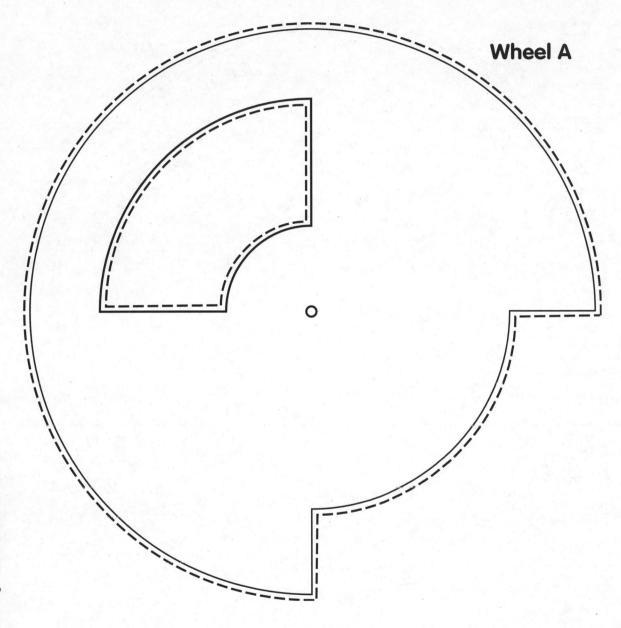

*Early Themes: Neighborhood and Community  Scholastic Professional Books*

# Science in My Community

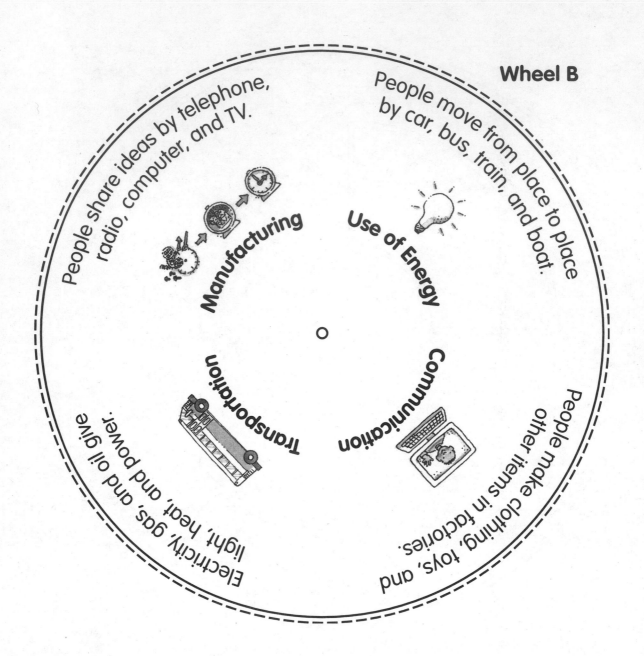

People share ideas by telephone, radio, computer, and TV.

People move from place to place by car, bus, train, and boat.

Manufacturing

Use of Energy

Transportation

Communication

Electricity, gas, and oil give light, heat, and power.

People make clothing, toys, and other items in factories.

*Early Themes: Neighborhood and Community* Scholastic Professional Books

# Our Errand Lists

## My Errand List

Buy milk.

_____

Get gas for the car.

_____

Get a haircut.

_____

Buy a loaf of bread.

_____

Take dance lessons.

_____

## My Errand List

Mail a letter.

_____

Borrow a book.

_____

Buy an apple.

_____

Have my teeth cleaned.

_____

Learn to read and write.

_____

## My Errand List

Mail a package.

_____

Put money in savings.

_____

Get my sore throat checked.

_____

Buy a basketball.

_____

Buy an ice cream cone.

_____

## My Errand List

Buy one dozen eggs.

_____

Get my bike repaired.

_____

Pick up a sandwich.

_____

Buy a box of cereal.

_____

Learn to add and subtract.

_____

*Early Themes: Neighborhood and Community* Scholastic Professional Books

# Getting Around

I have somewhere to go
And I already know
There are many good ways to get there.
A train, bus, or car
Would take me quite far,
Or I might fly a plane in the air.
A boat would be nice
Or my skates on the ice
Or my bicycle. That would work, too.
There are so many ways
I might travel these days.
If you were me, what would you do?

—Kathleen M. Hollenbeck

*Early Themes: Neighborhood and Community*  Scholastic Professional Books

# People Live and Work in a Community

**M**ost young children recognize the need for community workers such as police officers, veterinarians, and waiters. In this section, children will identify a host of community workers by role and learn how those workers help provide goods and services within a community. Children will also consider their own responsibilities toward their communities and examine the need for and function of community leaders.

### BACKGROUND NOTES

The success of a community depends on the contributions of its members. Each person's contribution is important, no matter how small. Young children should be aware of this and encouraged to look for ways to help others—for example, carrying a grocery bag in from the car. Small deeds will someday lead to greater ones.

# I Need You!

**Children assume the roles of community workers and invite their classmates to be the people or animals who need them.**

## Teaching the Lesson

**1** Secretly assign each child the role of a community worker. (See list, below.)

**2** Let children stand before the class and identify the role they're playing. For example, a child might say, "I am a veterinarian. Who needs me?"

**3** Classmates raise their hands and pretend to be various people or animals who would need such a helper—for example, "I am a cat. I need you." Each child will play the role of only one worker, but many children may respond as the people or animals in need.

### Community Workers

| | |
|---|---|
| Baker | Lifeguard |
| Banker | Letter Carrier |
| Bus Driver | News Anchor |
| Car Mechanic | Reporter |
| Chef | Nurse |
| Dairy Farmer | Painter |
| Dancer | Park Ranger |
| Dentist | Pilot |
| Doctor | Police Officer |
| Firefighter | Singer |
| Florist | Softball Coach |
| Cashier | Teacher |
| Hair Stylist | Veterinarian |
| Lawyer | Waiter |
| Librarian | Writer |

**ACTIVITY Extension** Share the poem "Ice Cream Man." (See below.) Give each child one "van" cut from paper. Have children paint their vans to advertise something they would have fun selling to others.

**Ice Cream Man**
If I were old enough to drive,
I'd be an ice cream man.
I'd paint delicious
ice cream colors
on my ice cream van.
My bell would clang,
a loud, loud clang
up and down the streets.
When kids came running,
I'd have fun
selling ice cream treats.

—Sandra Liatsos

**Literature Connection** Build children's appreciation for just about any career by bringing in books from the Neighborhood series, such as Alice K. Flanagan's *Mr. Yee Fixes Cars* (Children's Press, 1998). Dozens of titles explore the jobs of community workers from firefighters to farmers.

## Learning Center Link

*What would your students like to be when they grow up? Place a covered box in the learning center, along with a stack of scrap paper. Have children write their names and desired careers on pieces of paper and drop their answers in the box. At week's end, graph the results.*

# Who Is the Helper?

**Children solve riddles to identify community workers.**

## Materials

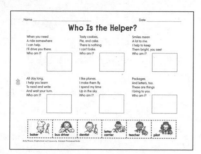

- ◎ "Who Is the Helper?" reproducible (page 40)
- ◎ scissors
- ◎ glue

## Teaching the Lesson

1. Give each child a copy of page 40. Read each riddle together. Have children raise their hands if they know which worker each describes.

2. Have children cut out the squares at the bottom of the page and glue each one in place beside the riddle that describes the helper shown.

**ACTIVITY Extension** Hold a career week. Each day, invite three parents or other people from the community to visit your classroom and talk with children about their careers. Take a photo of each guest. Have children take turns creating a page about each guest for a class "Careers in Our Community" book. They can glue the photo to a sheet of sturdy paper, along with information about the person and career.

**Literature Connection** Children will love reading and solving the riddles in *What's My Job?*, a Hello Reader book by Lyn Calder (Scholastic, 2000). Encourage children to take turns reading the riddles aloud for classmates to solve.

# Learning Center Link

*Place clay in the learning center, and invite children to create miniature community workers. Designate a display area for finished miniatures. Provide folded place cards on which children can label their workers and briefly describe what they do.*

# Who Can Help?

**Children sort playing cards to match community workers with the needs they fill.**

## Materials

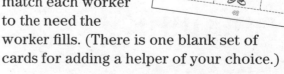

- ◎ "Who Can Help?" reproducibles (pages 41–42)
- ◎ scissors

## Teaching the Lesson

1. Give each child a copy of pages 41 and 42. Have children cut apart the cards and match each worker to the need the worker fills. (There is one blank set of cards for adding a helper of your choice.)

2. Divide the class into pairs, and suggest that each pair use one set of cards to play Go Fish. Partners will take turns requesting cards from each other, matching workers with needs and trying to get as many pairs as possible.

Encourage children to use the cards to play additional games, such as Memory, in which children lay the cards facedown and turn over two at a time to try to match needs with workers.

**Literature Connection** Read Eileen Spinelli's heartwarming story, *Somebody Loves You, Mr. Hatch* (Bradbury Press, 1991). After reading the story, talk with students about the importance of belonging and being appreciated—at home, at school, and in one's neighborhood or community. Discuss the ways people in a community can show concern or appreciation for one another— for example, by baking cookies, bringing flowers, or making cards.

## Learning Center Link

*Leave notepaper, stickers, markers, crayons, and pencils in the learning center. Encourage children to make note cards to let a friend or family member know they care.*

LANGUAGE ARTS/ SOCIAL STUDIES

# Write to Community Workers

**Children write to community workers, thanking them in words and pictures for their efforts and asking questions about the work they do.**

## Materials

- chart paper
- colored paper
- stickers, glitter, and other craft items
- glue
- lined paper
- pencils

## Teaching the Lesson

1. On chart paper, help children list workers in their school, neighborhood, or community who make a difference in their lives.

2. Ask each child to choose one person in particular whom they would like to thank.

3. Help children fold colored paper in half and then use stickers, glitter, glue, and other craft items to make a decorative card for the person.

4. Glue lined paper inside the note cards and have children write or dictate a message of thanks.

**ACTIVITY Extension** Use the completed "Careers in Our Community" book (see Activity Extension, page 37) as a yellow pages of sorts. Give each child an index card on which you have written a problem, such as "Jason's new puppy is sick." Ask children to identify the need that arises from the problem and find the community worker in the book who can best satisfy that need. In this case, Jason needs a doctor to care for his pet, and a veterinarian would be that helper.

**Literature Connection** Virginia Kroll's *Pink Paper Swans* (William B. Eerdmans, 1994) offers a unique look at how one person can contribute to the life and well-being of another. After reading the story, cut the shape of a swan from pink paper. Make one for each child. Have children write on the swan the name of a person who has helped them learn to do something they deem important, such as play piano or ride a bike.

## Learning Center Link

*What impact do community leaders have on the lives of the people they represent? In the learning center, place a magnetic photo album in which you have displayed newspaper photographs of leaders in the local community. Beneath each photo, write the person's name, title, and a description of the job they do.*

SOCIAL STUDIES

# People in a Community Help Each Other

**Children notice the ways people in a community help each other, and consider ways they can help, too.**

## Teaching the Lesson

1. Invite children to think about times that they've needed the help of a family member, friend, or other person in the community.

2. Ask volunteers to share their stories with the class. For example, a child might say, "I fell and scraped my knee at the park. Mrs. Hall cleaned it for me and put on a bandage."

3. Talk about the importance of contributing to a community. Ask children to suggest ways they've helped or intend to help out in their community—for example, by picking up litter, conserving water, collecting canned food for a soup kitchen, or staying behind to help clean up after a community event.

4. Start a "We're Community Helpers" bulletin board. Let children add pictures and stories to it throughout the theme unit to show how they help in their communities.

**ACTIVITY Extension** Brainstorm ways your class can do something to help the community. Vote on one and do it! Consider instituting an ongoing class-service project. Students can choose one for a year-long focus or vote on a new project each month.

**Literature Connection** *Grandpa's Corner Store*, by DyAnne DiSalvo-Ryan (HarperCollins, 2000), highlights the warmth and generosity of neighbors as they rally to help save a family-owned business. Use the story as a springboard for a discussion of how people can make a difference in the lives of others by showing support, compassion, and faith.

## Learning Center Link

*Stock your learning center with various picture books that demonstrate caring and compassion in a community. One stellar example is Patricia Polacco's Chicken Sunday (Philomel Books, 1992).*

Name _____

Date _____

# Who Is the Helper?

When you need
A ride somewhere
I can help.
I'll drive you there.
Who am I?

Tasty cookies,
Pie, and cake.
There is nothing
I can't bake.
Who am I?

Smiles mean
A lot to me.
I help to keep
Them bright, you see!
Who am I?

All day long,
I help you learn
To read and write
And wait your turn.
Who am I?

I like planes.
I make them fly.
I spend my time
Up in the sky.
Who am I?

Packages
And letters, too.
These are things
I bring to you.
Who am I?

 **baker**

 **bus driver**

**dentist**

 **letter carrier**

 **teacher**

 **pilot**

40

*Early Themes: Neighborhood and Community* Scholastic Professional Books

# Who Can Help?

| | | |
|---|---|---|
| I help keep people healthy. | I protect people from crime. | I put out fires. |
| I sell food to people. | I find good books. | I fix cars. |
| I help children learn sports. | I help keep swimmers safe. | |

Early Themes: Neighborhood and Community  Scholastic Professional Books

# Who Can Help?

*Early Themes: Neighborhood and Community*  Scholastic Professional Books

# Celebrate Neighborhoods and Communities

**W**rap-up your unit on neighborhoods and communities with hands-on activities designed to assess and reinforce what the children have learned. Children will adopt the roles of community workers and set up their own community in the classroom. They'll play games centered on the community theme and use the pullout poster provided to create and solve location riddles.

### BACKGROUND NOTES

Children's expression in role-play and success in creating a realistic community atmosphere provide valid tools for assessment. Observe the way your students interact and the range of workers they represent. Do they have a clear understanding of each worker's role? Do they comprehend their interdependence and their importance to the workings of the community?

# Turn Your Classroom Into a Neighborhood

**Children create a neighborhood in the classroom, and role-play community workers such as bakers, store owners, and librarians.**

## Materials

◎ construction paper

◎ markers

◎ masking or cellophane tape

## Teaching the Lesson

1. Tell children that they are going to make their own community in the classroom. Ask children to name community workers and jobs to include.

2. Invite each child to choose the position of a community worker. Encourage diversity in their choices.

3. Have children make signs that represent what they do and tape them to the front of their desks.

4. Let children reposition their desks to arrange the community as they wish.

5. Find fun ways to use the community— for example, invite another class in for a tour while children pretend to do their jobs. Provide craft materials and let children make products or tools that correspond to their jobs—for example, paper cookies and muffins for a baker. Allow children to take turns being patrons, business owners, and so on.

 **ACTIVITY Extension** Make community bingo cards. Draw 12 squares on a sheet of 8½- by 11-inch paper. In each square, draw pictures of the jobs children have selected. (You can use the picture cards on page 42 for some of the jobs.) Create several different versions of the cards, as well as a separate picture card for each job. Photocopy and distribute the cards and bingo markers. Then turn over picture cards at random and have children mark their cards accordingly until they cover five jobs in a row.

# Design Your Own Home

**Children draw a home on paper. Their home will be imaginary but should reflect their own personality, culture, wants, needs, family size, and so on.**

## Materials

◎ drawing paper

◎ crayons

## Teaching the Lesson

1. Invite children to close their eyes and imagine the home of their dreams. What would it look like? What color would it be? How many floors would it have? Where would the kitchen be? How would they get up and down stairs? What fun and exciting features would it have inside and out?

2. Give children drawing paper, and ask them to design a home of their own choosing. As they create, encourage them to consider their own likes/dislikes, meal habits, sleep habits, family size, color preferences, and so on.

3. Invite volunteers to share and explain their finished designs.

**Literature Connection** Share Melissa Bay Mathis's delightful *Animal House* (Simon & Schuster, 1999) for an enchanting look at what makes a perfect home.

## ART/LANGUAGE ARTS

# Colors in My Community

**Children and their families explore their own community to find examples of items that are red, orange, yellow, green, blue, and other colors.**

## Materials

◎ "Colors in My Community" reproducible (page 47)

Name_____ Date_____

### Colors in My Community

I see colors everywhere
In my community.
Here is where I find them.
This is what I see.

| Color | Where I See It |
|-------|----------------|
| Red | |
| Orange | |
| Yellow | |
| Green | |
| Blue | |
| Purple | |
| Brown | |
| Black | |
| White | |

## Teaching the Lesson

1. Give each child a copy of page 47. Have children take home the activity and enlist their family's help in finding objects, buildings, or other things in the community that match the colors listed.

2. Encourage children to bring completed pages back to school. Use them to add community words to the word wall.

3. Try the same activity, this time having children look for numbers in their community. Have children complete a record sheet to show places they see the numbers 1–10. For example, they might find the numbers 2 and 5 on a speed limit sign, or the numbers 1 and 7 on an exit sign. When children return their papers to school, talk about what the numbers mean in each case and how they help people.

**ACTIVITY Extension** Shapes surround us, in the most unlikely places! Send children and their families on a shape search in their own community, where they may see yield signs as triangles, stop signs as hexagons, and windows as circles or squares. Have them find two examples for each of the following shapes: circle, square, triangle, hexagon, and rectangle. Ask them to keep an eye open for hard-to-find shapes, such as a pentagon, octagon, or diamond. For another extension, challenge children and their families to find objects or places in the community that start with the letters of the alphabet from A to Z.

**Literature Connection** For a lighthearted look at places in the community, read Mercer Mayer's *Little Monster's Neighborhood* (Golden Press, 1978).

# Teaching With the Poster:

# I Am a Community Helper

This pocket-chart poster (bound in the center of the book) presents six community helpers and the jobs they do. As children read and complete the simple poem, they will match words and pictures and identify specific functions of community helpers.

**I Am a Community Helper!**

I help people every day.

I am a _____ , you see.

When people want a _____ ,

They often call on me.

| doctor | hairstylist | shoe seller |
| librarian | baker | pilot |
| haircut | pair of shoes | checkup |
| muffin | plane ride | book |

SCHOLASTIC

1. Cut apart the sentence strips and cards on the poster. Laminate for durability. Arrange the lines of the poem in order in the top half of the pocket chart. Display the words and pictures in the bottom half.

2. Read aloud the rhyme to students. Choose a volunteer to select a helper card (word or picture card) and place it over the first blank line. Continue reading, letting the same volunteer find the words that describe what that helper provides for people and place that card over the second blank line.

3. Reread the poem with students. Then remove the cards and repeat the procedure, placing other helpers and their responsibilities in the blanks.

4. Extend the activity by asking students to sort the cards by who sells an item that people can buy (baker, sales clerk) and who offers a service that someone needs or wants to have done for them (doctor, hair stylist, plumber, pilot).

5. Use 3- by 5-inch index cards to make new cards for other community helpers. (See suggestions, below.) You might have students focus on workers in one field at a time: helpers in their school (teacher, principal, nurse, librarian), safety workers in the community (crossing guards, police officers, firefighters, emergency medics), and so on.

## COMMUNITY HELPERS

architect, babysitter, day care provider, musician, actor, conductor, jeweler, singer, repair person, flight attendant, waiter, coach, animal trainer, clown, security guard, mechanic, ice cream vendor, umpire, delivery person, sanitation worker

## Learning Center Link

*Let students use the pocket-chart poem on the poster to make mini-books about community helpers. Stock the learning center with copies of page 48. Have students cut apart the mini-book pages and complete them for new community helpers, filling in the missing words and adding illustrations. Students can complete a set of mini-book pages (2) for each community helper they wish to feature in their books.*

# Colors in My Community

I see colors everywhere
In my community.
Here is where I find them.
This is what I see.

| Color | Where I See It |
|---|---|
| Red | |
| Orange | |
| Yellow | |
| Green | |
| Blue | |
| Purple | |
| Brown | |
| Black | |
| White | |

# I Am a Community Helper

I help people every day.
I am a _____
you see.

When people want a
_____,
they often call on me.

I help people every day.
I am a _____
you see.

When people want a
_____,
they often call on me.

*Early Themes: Neighborhood and Community*  Scholastic Professional Books